LET'S PLAY SOLDIER, GEORGE WASHINGTON!

BY PETER AND CONNIE ROOP

D0107104

SCHOLASTIC INC.

New York   Toronto   London   Auckland   Sydney
Mexico City   New Delhi   Hong Kong   Buenos Aires

ISBN 0-439-43924-8

12 11 10 9 8 7 6 5 4 3 2 1   2 3 4 5 6 7/0

Printed in the U.S.A.   40
First printing, September 2002

For Mother,
who has always set
a wonderful example
with her own rules
of civility

Table of Contents

INTRODUCTION

George Washington is famous. He was General Washington. He was President Washington.

General Washington led our American army to victory in the Revolutionary War. How did George become such a good general?

President Washington was our first President. Why did Americans trust George so much that they elected him to lead our newborn country?

George Washington had no children of his own. Why is he called the Father of Our Country?

General Washington bravely crossed the icy Delaware River. How did he learn to survive such hardships?

George Washington fought a war so Americans could be free. But he also owned hundreds of slaves.

We celebrate George Washington's birthday in February on Presidents' Day. But did you know George Washington really had two birthdays?

George Washington's face is on every dollar bill. Why isn't he smiling?

The answers to these questions lie in who George Washington was as a boy and as a young man.

This book is about George Washington before he made history.

1

GEORGE WASHINGTON IS BORN

February 11, 1732. Cherry blossoms bloomed. Fat red robins hunted fat red worms. Warm winds blew over Wakefield Farm in Virginia. A baby cried. His mother, Mary, rocked him, and the baby smiled.

Gus, the baby's father, opened the family Bible to the birth page and dipped his turkey feather pen into black ink. Very carefully, he wrote that his son was born at ten o'clock that morning. He proudly wrote the baby's name and the date.

George Washington
February 11, 1732

The first Washington came to America from England in 1657. His name was

John Washington. John was George's great-grandfather. John married the daughter of a wealthy tobacco planter. He soon owned five thousand acres of land. John joined Virginia's militia and became the first Colonel Washington.

George's grandfather Lawrence Washington also grew tobacco. He bought more land. He believed that the more land a man owned, the richer he was.

Lawrence worked hard in Virginia's government. He believed in the Washington family motto, "By their deeds so shall ye know them."

George's father, Gus, was just like his father and grandfather. He bought land. He grew tobacco. The brown tobacco leaves were like money for Gus Washington. He shipped them across the Atlantic Ocean to England. The tobacco was traded for tools, nails, rope, clothes, guns, axes, books, glass, furniture, paper, needles, knives, pins, and other things Gus needed in America.

Gus Washington owned slaves. They did

the hard work of planting, weeding, and harvesting his tobacco plants. They cooked, cleaned, and washed clothes. Many farmers in Virginia owned slaves. Without slaves, the farmers said, they could not support their families.

In 1715, Gus married Jane Butler. She was sixteen years old. They built Wakefield House, where George was born.

Gus and Jane had three children: Lawrence, Augustine, and baby Jane. Gus grew rich. He wanted his sons to have a good English education. Gus took them to school in England. There, Gus met yellow-haired Mary Ball from Virginia. Mary was visiting her family in England. Gus liked Mary's independent spirit.

Sadly, while Gus was away, his wife, Jane, died. Gus was lonely. His boys were still in England. He had young Jane to care for.

He met Mary Ball again. Mary loved to ride fast horses. Gus enjoyed watching Mary. She seemed to like horses more than people. But Gus liked her.

In 1731, Gus married Mary Ball. Mary joined Gus and six-year-old Jane at Wakefield.

On February 11, 1732, George Washington was born. For a month, Mary carried healthy baby George around to show him off to friends and family. Everyone loved smiling baby George Washington.

George Washington's first home was the redbrick Wakefield House. Wakefield stood on the banks of a creek. It had three bedrooms. There was a dining room, a kitchen, and an attic. The cabins of the Washingtons' slaves were near the fields.

George Washington lived at Wakefield until he was three years old. He learned to walk and talk there. He watched horses galloping. He watched dogs, pigs, children, and chickens running. He watched slaves working. He watched ships being loaded and unloaded on the Potomac River.

George had many friends from nearby farms. He laughed and played with them in the meadows and in the woods.

2
GEORGE'S TWO NEW HOMES

The Washington family outgrew Wake-field. In 1733, George's baby sister, Elizabeth, was born. Gus wrote her name in the family Bible. In 1734, Gus wrote the name of George's new brother, Samuel.

The next year, the Washingtons moved fifty miles to a farm in the wilderness. George watched the slaves load tools, animals, and furniture onto big rafts. The slaves pushed the rafts up the river to the new farm, Little Hunting Creek.

George loved Little Hunting Creek. Deer, bears, wolves, foxes, raccoons, and turkeys lived in the woods. Geese, swans, eagles, and ducks filled the air. The wide, slow Potomac River flowed nearby. There were fish to catch and animals to watch. George played with Jane, Elizabeth, and Sam in the fields and forests. He played with the slave children, too.

Gus built a dock on the river. George loved to fish off the dock. All his life, fishing was one of his favorite hobbies.

That same year, Jane died from a fever. George was sad. He missed his big sister. Soon, young George had other children to play with. Jack Washington was born in 1736 and Charles in 1738.

In the summer when he was five, George had a big surprise. His stepbrothers, Lawrence and Augustine, came home from England. Lawrence was fourteen years older than George. He was tall, intelligent, and had good manners. Lawrence was George's hero. Lawrence liked George, too. He enjoyed his company and his good thinking. George said Lawrence was his best friend.

George turned six years old in 1738. He lost some baby teeth. His adult teeth grew in straight and strong.

Gus decided to move again. He bought Ferry Farm. Gus now owned more than ten thousand acres of land. Mildred Washington was born at Ferry Farm in 1739. But she died before she was a year old.

George enjoyed Ferry Farm. There were new woods to explore. He could ride to new places and meet new neighbors.

George grew tall. His hands and feet were large. His arms were strong from wrestling, cutting wood, and throwing rocks. His legs were strong from running and riding. Sometimes George seemed shy, but everyone liked him.

Mary Washington was busy with her babies. She told George to play with Elizabeth and Sam. They raced across the fields. They wrestled in the grass. They played chase around the meadow. They went fishing and boating. Because he was the biggest and oldest, George was in charge. Something about young George Washington made his brothers and sister listen to him. Maybe it was his voice. Maybe it was his deep blue eyes. Maybe it was his reddish brown hair. Maybe it was how he behaved himself. Maybe it was how he took command of their games. Elizabeth, Samuel, Jack, and Charles eagerly followed their big brother George.

George Washington loved to learn. The first thing he learned was how to ride horses. His father lifted George onto a horse. George held onto the horse's mane. He walked the horse around the farm. When George was older, he held the horse's reins. He galloped around the farm. George raced horses in the meadow and down dusty roads.

George learned how to hunt. He was very strong. He could easily lift a heavy gun. George often brought home deer, turkeys, and ducks for the hungry Washingtons. Meat was eaten at every meal. In Virginia, people ate meat five times a day!

George watched his father take notes. Gus wrote down how many barrels of tobacco he sold. He wrote down how much he was paid

for each barrel. He wrote down the names and values of his slaves. George liked the numbers his father added and subtracted.

George learned how to plant and harvest. Gus grew grain, fruit, and vegetables to feed the Washingtons and their slaves. George watched and helped out. For all of his life, George Washington loved to grow things.

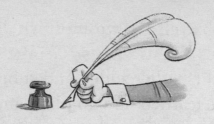

3
GEORGE LEARNS MANY LESSONS

George wished he could go to school in England like his stepbrothers, Lawrence and Augustine. But with the new, bigger farm, Gus did not have enough money to send George to England.

When he was seven years old, George probably went to school. But no one knows for sure.

Either at school or at home, George learned to read and write. George dipped his quill pen into ink. He did not let the ink drip onto his paper. He wrote his letters slowly and carefully, just like he did most things. George spelled by writing the sounds he heard. He did this all of his life. He wrote *lye* for lie, *oyl* for oil, and *blew* for blue.

George wrote in notebooks. He filled the pages with words, numbers, and pictures. He wrote about famous people. He wrote about history. All his life, George would write journals and letters.

George especially enjoyed numbers. He could add, subtract, multiply, and divide. He kept good records, like his father did. He wrote bills to be paid. George knew what people owed him to the penny.

George enjoyed counting. He counted windows, rows of plants, and barrels of tobacco. He counted logs in a pile and steps around a field. He once counted 71,000 seeds in a pound of red clover!

When he was eight, George learned about war. In 1740, England was at war with Spain. Lawrence Washington followed family tradition and joined the English army. He was Captain Washington. George admired Lawrence

in his red pants, blue coat, and hat with gold trim.

George missed Lawrence when he was in the war. George liked reading Lawrence's letters about the battles he was in. George Washington and his friends played soldiers. George was the general. His soldier friends marched behind General Washington in make-believe battles.

George decided he would be a soldier, like Lawrence. No more make-believe fighting. George Washington would be a real soldier. Maybe he would even be a real general someday!

Lawrence came home. He told George about his battles. George did not like Lawrence's bad cough. Lawrence had gotten sick during the war. His cough would not go away.

In 1743, George's world turned upside down. His father died. George was only eleven years old. George Washington's life would never be the same again.

In his will, Gus gave Little Hunting Creek

Farm to Lawrence. Lawrence changed the name. His hero during the war had been Admiral Edward Vernon. Lawrence named his farm Mount Vernon.

Augustine got Wakefield, the next biggest farm. This was where George had been born. George, Gus's third son, got Ferry Farm. George could not own it until he turned twenty-one years old. George's mother, Mary, would run his farm. Mary worried about money. How could she run such a big farm? George wanted to help, but he was only eleven.

Mary Washington had a strong temper. These days, she suddenly grew angry for no reason. She yelled at the slaves. She would not let anyone, not even George, ride her favorite horses. George disobeyed her. He accidentally killed one of her best horses. His mother never forgave him.

George was unhappy at Ferry Farm. He often rode (on a poor horse) to Mount Vernon to see Lawrence. The two brothers became even better friends. George enjoyed

Lawrence's friends. Many had gone to school in England. They had fine manners. They ran big plantations. They danced. They went on foxhunts. George wanted to be like them. He wished he could go to school in England.

4

GEORGE TEACHES HIMSELF

But George knew he could not go to school in England. He wrote down rules to make himself a better person. He wrote 110 rules of conduct for himself. George followed these rules all his life.

George liked to be fair. One of his rules said, "At Play . . . it's Good manners to Give Place to the last Commer [person to come]." He also wrote, "Keep your Nails clean and short, also your Hands and Teeth Clean." All his life, George tried to keep his own teeth clean. But his teeth and gums often hurt.

George wanted to have good table manners. He wrote, "Keep your fingers clean and when foul wipe them on a Corner of your Table Napkin."

George wrote rules about minding your own business, being polite and kind to others, and not swearing. George had a strong temper, like his mother. He wrote down ways to control his temper. George wanted to be honest. He wrote, "Be Carefull to keep your Promise."

George did not want to own just Ferry Farm when he was older. He wanted more land and more money. He wanted people to look up to him as an important person.

George worked hard to become a Virginia gentleman. He became a good dancer. He listened to music. He learned how to fight with swords. He read and studied more. He watched Lawrence's friends. He listened politely to what they had to say. George talked only when he was sure of himself. George loved foxhunting and galloping through fields and forests on strong, fast horses. He became a better rider.

One day, George decided to move to Mount Vernon. Ferry Farm was too small for strong-minded George and strong-willed

Mary. But all his life, George treated his mother with respect.

Living at Mount Vernon was wonderful for George. He could hunt, ride, and meet important people almost every day.

George kept up his schoolwork. Lawrence knew George was good in math. He told George to learn how to survey land. Surveying was making a map of the land so people knew where its borders were. Surveying was a valuable skill. More farms were being cut into the Virginia wilderness. A good surveyor could make money and buy the best land.

George found his father's surveying tools. He practiced with them. When he was fourteen, George made a map of the turnip field at Mount Vernon. He carefully wrote down the number of acres. He drew a compass to show direction. He drew the borders around the edge. He proudly signed his turnip field map *GW.*

One day, Lawrence Washington married beautiful Anne Fairfax. Her father, Colonel William Fairfax, owned a farm near Mount

Vernon. He was one of the richest men in all the thirteen colonies.

Colonel Fairfax liked George. He saw how hard George worked and studied. He watched George ride fast horses. He saw how people liked strong, thoughtful George Washington.

Colonel Fairfax knew George wanted to make his way in the world. Colonel Fairfax said he would help George get into the English navy. George could travel and have adventures. He might even get rich capturing enemy ships!

George was excited. This was his chance to make a name for himself! He told Colonel Fairfax he would join the navy. But first, he had to get his mother's permission.

Mary Washington said yes! George was surprised. He packed his bags. Then, his mother changed her mind. She said no, he could not join the navy. George was disappointed. He argued with his mother. He probably forgot some of his 110 rules of conduct.

Mary said she would write to her brother in England for advice. Nine long months later, the answer arrived from England. Mary's brother said joining the navy was a bad idea. George would get very little pay. He would be treated like a dog or even a slave. Imagine how history would have changed if George Washington had become an English sailor instead of an American soldier!

George was fifteen years old. Anne and Lawrence took George to visit Anne's parents. George met more Virginia gentlemen and ladies. He carefully followed his 110 rules of conduct. Everyone was impressed with polite, quiet, athletic George Washington.

5
GEORGE GETS HIS FIRST JOB

One day, a man from England came to Virginia. His name was Lord Fairfax, and he was Anne's father's cousin.

Lord Fairfax owned more land in Virginia than any other person. He owned more than five million acres! His land stretched west into the wilderness. Lord Fairfax came to America to visit his land. He wanted to know what he owned. He wanted the land divided into farms he could sell.

Anne, Lawrence, and George visited Lord Fairfax. George liked Lord Fairfax. Lord Fairfax liked George. He invited George to go foxhunting with him. Lord Fairfax saw that George was an excellent rider. George was

polite. George was also a very good land sur
veyor.

Lord Fairfax wanted his land surveyed.
James Genn was in charge of the surveying
team and would need help. Lord Fairfax decided to take a chance. Who could be better
than strong, skilled George Washington?

George was only sixteen. Now, he had his
first job. He would map Lord Fairfax's wilderness lands.

And his mother said George could go!

In March 1748, the men set off. George
took a big step toward becoming the Father
of His Country.

The trip to Lord Fairfax's land lasted thirty
days. As usual, George learned many things.
The first day, the men rode forty miles. Spring
was in the air. Flowers bloomed. Streams ran
fast and cold. George enjoyed the woods. He
liked the land.

The men slept outside seventeen nights in
a row. (George counted.) During the day, they
surveyed. They worked fast. They worked

in rain and shine. They climbed steep hills. They mapped long valleys. They watched for rattlesnakes.

George liked the hard work. He liked being outside. He did not mind carrying the heavy thirty-three-foot iron chain. He liked sitting around the fire at night, listening to stories.

One chilly night, George fell asleep by the fire. Suddenly, his straw bed burst into flames. George was lucky. A friend put out the fire before George was burned.

George enjoyed his adventures. He liked living outside in good and bad weather. George made up his mind to become the best surveyor in Virginia. He could get land and make money.

The surveying job ended. With money in his pocket, George rode home to Ferry Farm. George lived at Ferry Farm for the next year. He grew food and tobacco. He read, studied, and wrote in his notebooks. He surveyed. He visited friends. He took dancing lessons. He tried not to argue with his mother.

But the land at Ferry Farm was poor. George wanted more in his life than to scratch out a living on a poor farm. He wanted to live like Lawrence and his rich friends. *How can I reach this goal?* George asked himself.

George's hard work paid off. In 1749, he became county surveyor. People heard about this hardworking, honest surveyor. He got more surveying jobs.

In three years, George made more than two hundred land surveys. (He counted.) Most times, George was paid in money. Sometimes, he was paid in land. Best of all, the money he made helped him leave Ferry Farm. He was on his own. He was out from under his mother's watchful eyes.

While he worked, George looked for good land to buy. When he was eighteen, George Washington owned almost fifteen hundred acres of the best land in Virginia. His dream of a better life was coming true.

6
GEORGE JOINS THE ARMY

George often visited Lawrence. Lawrence's cough was worse. Lawrence decided to go to a warm place. Maybe there his cough would get better. He asked George to go with him.

In 1751, the Washington brothers sailed to Barbados. The voyage lasted thirty-seven days. (George counted.) It stormed. George was seasick for ten days. The bread had bugs in it. George fished for food and fun. He used his math skills to see where they were.

George watched the tough sailors do their jobs. He enjoyed their stories. He liked these gruff men. They liked curious George.

Maybe I should be a sailor after all, George thought.

George liked Barbados. He made new

friends. He went to parties and dances. He counted ships. He explored.

One night, George had a bad headache. He could not sleep. He was hot. He was cold. He had sores on his body and his face. George wrote in his journal that he was "strongly attacked with the smallpox." Almost everyone who got smallpox died. George thought he might die, too.

George was sick for four weeks. Finally, his fever ended. He had scars on his face from the sores. But he was alive! It was good that George had gotten smallpox. It meant that he could never get it again.

George told Lawrence he had to go home. He had to do some surveys. George sailed to Virginia. George took important letters to Governor Dinwiddie in Williamsburg, the capital of the Virginia colony.

Governor Dinwiddie liked George Washington. George liked the governor. George rested for a few days before going home. He saw his mother. He surveyed. He bought 552 more acres of land.

George went to Mount Vernon. Anne had bad news about Lawrence. He was still sick. But he was coming home!

George was excited to see Lawrence again. But his brother was worse. Lawrence said that when he died, Mount Vernon would belong to Anne and their little daughter, Sarah. If Sarah died, George would own Mount Vernon. George did not want Mount Vernon. He wanted Lawrence to live. George was with Lawrence when he died. George was sad. His best friend, his special big brother, was dead.

George would have to make his way in the world on his own now. He was twenty years old.

Lawrence's job in the Virginia militia was open. Governor Dinwiddie remembered capable George Washington. He gave George the job. Major George Washington was very proud of his new uniform.

George turned twenty-one on February 22, 1753. George had been born on February 11, 1732. But in 1752, the calendars were changed. This is because the old calendar

was off by eleven days. Now, George's birthday was February 22. Some years, when he wanted to, George celebrated his birthday twice! On his birthday, George inherited Ferry Farm. But his mother would not let him have it for many more years.

George also inherited ten slaves and 2,291 acres. George now owned more than five thousand acres of land.

That year, England and France became enemies. England claimed land west of the Appalachian Mountains. But the French claimed this land, too. They built forts on it. They told the English to keep out.

The English wrote a letter telling the French to leave. But who would dare take the letter to the French? It would be very dangerous. The man would have to live in the woods for months. He would have to go through Native American lands. Many Native Americans were friends of the French.

Governor Dinwiddie remembered George Washington. George was young. He was strong and tough. He knew how to live in the wilderness. He was a major in the army.

George raced to Governor Dinwiddie. He would take the letter to the French! He would return with their answer!

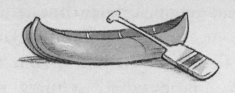

7

GEORGE SURVIVES
THE WILDERNESS

In October 1753, Major George Washington set off with six men. Leaves fell. Rain fell. George led the men over mountains. He led them across rivers and streams. George studied the land. He wrote in his journal. He counted fourteen days of rain or snow.

They stopped where two rivers came together. (Pittsburgh is there today.) George knew it was a good place for a fort.

Finally, the men reached the French fort. George put on his best uniform. George gave the letter to the French. The French said they would have an answer the next day.

George did not waste his time. He walked

around the French fort. He counted the buildings. He measured the tall walls. He made a map of the fort. He counted nine cannons, more than a hundred soldiers, and 220 canoes.

The next day, the French told George that the land belonged to them. Any Englishmen on their land would be arrested. They told George to take their message to Governor Dinwiddie.

There was nothing more Major Washington could do. It was the week before Christmas. George wanted to go home. The French helped. They gave the Englishmen two canoes and food.

For seven days, Washington and his men sped down icy rivers in their canoes. One canoe was wrecked during the trip.

George had to get the French answer to Governor Dinwiddie. He decided to walk hundreds of miles home. Christopher Gist went with him. George left his precious uniform. He wore deerskin clothes. He carried his rifle and a knapsack.

Washington and Gist hurried over the rivers and through the woods. The first day they walked eighteen miles. George had bad blisters on his feet. He put up with the pain.

One day, they walked for twenty-four hours without stopping. They came to a big river. Ice floated on it. It was too cold to swim across. They had one small ax. All day, they slowly chopped down trees. They made a small raft and two poles. They pushed the raft into the river. Ice hit the raft. George tried to stop the raft with his pole. He couldn't. George wrote in his journal that the pole "Jirk'd me into 10 Feet [of] Water but fortunately I saved my Self by catching hold of one of the raft logs." Using his strong arms, he pulled himself back onto the raft.

George and Christopher waded to an island. All night, they huddled in their cold, wet clothes. They had no tent. They had little food. They could not build a fire. That night the temperature fell below freezing. Gist's fingers froze. *Would they die in the wilderness?* George worried.

In the morning, George had a surprise. The river had frozen! They walked safely to the other shore. They found help at a settler's cabin. They bought horses. They rode fast.

Finally, on January 16, 1754, Major George Washington gave the French answer to Governor Dinwiddie. George had traveled more than a thousand miles! (He counted.) The governor promoted George from Major to Colonel.

Colonel Washington rode to Mount Vernon. George decided to write a book about his adventures. That way, more people would learn about his bravery and skills. George called his book *The Journal of Major George Washington . . . to the French Forces*. He told about the dangers and hardships he suffered. He told about the land. He drew a map.

George planned to farm now. But Governor Dinwiddie needed him again.

❽
George Starts a War and Surrenders for the Only Time in His Life

Governor Dinwiddie had sent men to build a fort in the wilderness. Colonel Washington was to take soldiers there and help them. Late in the summer of 1754, Colonel Washington and his 157 men marched west. George had no idea he was about to start a war with the French and Native Americans. The French and Indian War would last seven long, bloody years.

George and his men built a road in the wilderness. They cut down trees. They dug up rocks. They filled in holes. George desperately needed the road. He needed more men, food, guns, gunpowder, and cannons to fight the French. George learned that the French had built a fort exactly where he said the English fort should be!

Colonel Washington made up his mind. He would make the French leave their fort, even if it meant war. France and England were not at war. Yet.

One night, George and forty-six men (he counted them) slipped out of their camp. They knew French soldiers were near. The English found the French. Colonel Washington ordered an attack. The English fired. The French fired back. Soon the battle was over. The English had won!

One French soldier escaped. He raced to the fort and told about Washington's attack. The French were angry. This meant war! The French marched out to fight Washington.

On July 3, 1754, the French attacked. Bullets whistled like angry bees. Washington's soldiers fought hard. But there were too many French soldiers. George had a tough decision to make. He could keep fighting until all his men were dead. Or he could surrender and live to fight another day. He looked at his men. One hundred twenty-nine were dead or wounded. Colonel George Washington surrendered.

The French kept Washington's cannons, guns, and gunpowder. They told the English to walk back to Virginia. They made Washington and his men promise not to set foot on French land for a year. George Washington promised he would be back.

On July 4, 1754, Colonel Washington and his men headed home on the road they had built. George's bravery made him a hero to his men. He was a hero to English settlers in the forests.

George wrote to his brother Jack. He said, "I have heard bullets whistle and there is something charming in the sound."

Far away in England, King George II heard about George's bravery. The king was proud of this strong, brave English solider.

George went home to Mount Vernon. If he could not fight, George would farm.

9
GEORGE IS ALMOST KILLED!

But the English wanted revenge against the French. King George II sent General Edward Braddock to fight the French.

George could not miss this opportunity. As soon as he planted his crops, George joined General Braddock's army.

All his life, George Washington tried to keep his promises. He promised the French he would not set foot on their land for a year. But he could not miss getting revenge for his surrender! George broke his promise.

General Braddock liked George. He knew how brave he was. He saw how well George organized men. George liked General Braddock. The general was like a father to George. He taught George how to be a good general.

He shared his war books with George. He answered George's many questions. Each day George carefully copied the general's orders into his journal.

By June 1755, the English army was ready. They marched over George's road and into the wilderness. It was hard. The road was muddy, and the heavy wagons got stuck. Sometimes, the army only moved a half mile in a whole day!

George warned General Braddock. He said that in America, the French and their Native American friends fought differently than in Europe. They did not fight in open fields. They hid behind trees and rocks to fire their guns. General Braddock said he would fight like he did in Europe.

George suddenly got very sick. General Braddock thought George might die. He sent him to a doctor to be checked. George pestered the doctor. He did not want to miss any battles.

Finally, the doctor put George in a wagon and sent him back. When George made up his mind, it was nearly impossible to get him to change it.

George reached General Braddock late one afternoon. The general planned to attack the fort in the morning. George made it just in time!

On July 9, 1755, the English army marched through the thick woods toward the fort. George rode beside his hero, General Braddock. George could barely ride. He tied pillows onto his saddle to make the ride less bumpy.

The French and Native Americans waited until the English were spread out along the road. Then they attacked from behind trees and rocks. The English were trapped. George had been right!

Guns fired. Arrows flew. Hundreds of Englishmen died. General Braddock ordered his men to stay in line. He would not fight from behind rocks and trees.

But it was too late. The English soldiers were scared. They ran. The English army was soon in a big mess.

George and General Braddock were the only two officers left on their horses. More bullets whistled. More English died. General Braddock had five horses shot from beneath him. Still, he fought.

George begged the General to let him lead an attack against the French. The General said yes to his brave friend.

A bullet killed George's horse. George jumped onto another horse. That one was killed, too.

After the battle, George wrote his mother, "I had four bullet holes in my coat."

George Washington was very lucky. General Braddock was not so lucky. A bullet hit his chest. He ordered his men to keep fighting.

Soon, George was the only officer not killed or wounded. George kept fighting. He would not give up.

Finally, the sun set. The French had won!

Colonel Washington was disappointed. The French had defeated him twice. General

Braddock gave one last order. He wanted his friend George Washington to bury him.

On July 13, General Braddock died. George followed his last order. George learned a new lesson — bullets were not so charming, after all.

10
GEORGE WASHINGTON MAKES HISTORY

All his life, George Washington used the lessons he learned in his early life. George followed his 110 rules of conduct. He was polite, had good manners, and listened to others. He was clean and neat.

George surveyed and bought land. In 1793, George would draw a map of the five farms of Mount Vernon. Mount Vernon would have more than eight thousand acres. (George counted.)

On January 6, 1759, George married Martha Custis. Martha stood five feet tall. George stood six feet three inches tall.

Cheerful, energetic Martha looked up to her new husband. Martha often let George do things his way. But she could be as determined as George when she wanted something.

Martha's first husband had died. She had two children, Patsy and John. George became a father to Patsy and John. He loved them both very much. Martha owned land and one hundred fifty slaves. Under the law, when she married George, the land and slaves became his.

George felt he had to own slaves. He could not afford to pay people to work in his fields. Or repair his buildings. Or shoe his horses. Or take care of his house. George hoped someday all slaves would be free.

After he became President, George said, "I can clearly foresee that nothing but the rooting out of slavery can [save] our Union."

Sixty-two years later, President Abraham Lincoln led the fight to end slavery and save the Union. Guess who Abraham Lincoln's hero was when he was a young boy? Who President Lincoln's hero was when he was President? George Washington!

In his will, George Washington freed his slaves.

George worked hard to be a good farmer. Every day, he rode around Mount Vernon to check on things. He grew wheat and corn. George tried to grow or make everything he needed for Mount Vernon. He wanted Mount Vernon to be independent.

George worked hard for the Virginia government. Quietly, he helped make decisions that led to the colonies declaring independence from England. George's skills in the English army helped. He was chosen to be general.

General Washington led his soldiers through eight long years of war with England. George won some battles. He lost some battles. But General George Washington never surrendered.

General Washington led his troops to victory over England. A new nation was born — the United States of America.

The thirteen states needed a leader to unite them. People looked to George Washington. He watched over the creation of the Constitution of the United States.

In 1789, George Washington was elected the first President of the United States. He got all the votes!

In 1792, George was reelected President. Again, he got all the votes! George Washington is called the Father of His Country because he did so much to make us a nation.

George used his skills as a leader to guide the United States during its first years. He set such a good example that no president has ever outdone him.

Even though George was beloved by his countrymen, he rarely smiled. Why? Over the years, George's teeth hurt him more and more. He had teeth pulled and false teeth made. Some were made of elk teeth. Some were made of pig and cow teeth. Some were

human teeth. Some were made from hippopotamus teeth! One set of false teeth weighed three pounds. No wonder George Washington never smiled in his pictures!

George Washington retired to Mount Vernon in 1797. Finally, he was just Farmer Washington.

One cold, rainy day, George rode around the farm he loved so much. He got a very bad sore throat.

On December 14, 1799, George Washington died. He was only sixty-seven years old, but he had lived every year to the fullest.

One man wrote that George Washington was "First in war, first in peace, and first in the hearts of his countrymen." George Washington was famous throughout the world.

What George learned and did before he made history helped him become General Washington, President Washington, and Farmer Washington. Who would have guessed it on February 11, 1732?